# D[illegible]

Alan J. Frost

*All booklets are published thanks to the generous support of the members of the Catholic Truth Society*

CATHOLIC TRUTH SOCIETY
PUBLISHERS TO THE HOLY SEE

## Contents

## Introduction

Louis Marie de Montfort, like many seemingly 'destined' for sainthood, had a manner of life that was different, we might say other-worldly, from an early age. He grew to become an outstanding and passionate preacher of the message of the Rosary. He was also someone with a special calling, being occasionally blessed with the gift of prophecy. In his lifetime, he achieved over 10,000 conversions to the Faith, and from his great work, *'True Devotion To Mary'*[1], the Holy Father, Pope John Paul II takes his motto *'Totus Tuus'*, in honour of Our Blessed Lady. No less a person than Fr F.W. Faber (who translated *True Devotion*) had seen a divine inspiration in his work, and confidently predicted his canonisation (1947) back in the 1860's. Over 130 years later, in 1996, Pope John Paul II prayed at his tomb in St Laurent-sur-Sevre and proclaimed that St Louis Marie is to be placed among the leaders and guides of a spirituality which continues to animate the Church today.

---

[1] A popularised title, shortened from the reference to his work more fully known as *Treatise on True Devotion to the Blessed Virgin*. The title page of Montfort's study was missing when, having been lost, it was rediscovered in 1842.

One of the great saints of the Rosary is Louis Marie de Montfort, a saint directly in line from St Dominic and Blessed Alan de la Roche OP. He is known worldwide for his handy little book *'The Secret of the Rosary'*, giving guidance in the saying of the Rosary, and the important *'Love Of The Eternal Wisdom'*. He is perhaps less known for what is probably the greatest book on the Blessed Virgin Mary, *'True Devotion To Mary'*. Most popes have endorsed and promoted this study since its discovery in 1842. Indeed it is from this that Pope John Paul II takes his motto: *Totus Tuus* (*dedicated to Mary, meaning through Mary to Jesus*). The same pope, kneeling before the tomb of St Louis Marie in 1996, endorsed what he had already written, that Montfort is to be placed among the leaders and guides of a spirituality which animates the Church today.

Through all his trials and tribulations, and the depth and detail of his writings, the thrust of his teaching is that the simplest and fullest way to Jesus is through Mary: *ad Jesum per Mariam.*

## His Life

Louis Grignion de la Bachelarie was born on 31 January, 1673 in the village of Montfort-la-Cane, more commonly known as Montfort-sur-Meu, near Rennes in North-west France. He was the eldest of ten surviving children (several died in infancy), and his parents were of noble birth, though they were not well-off. He took the name 'Montfort' from the village of his birth, and the name Marie at his Confirmation, from a very early devotion to Our Lady. His humility, rather than humour, probably accounts for his adopting the name of his birthplace, for the name means Montfort of the Duck, a reference to an early legend.

From an early age, he showed a remarkable horror of sin, and a love of prayer. This would be displayed in formal settings and in solitary wanderings by streams and woods, singing *cantiques* to God he wrote himself even as a young boy. Recognising this exceptional devoutness in his son and the value of a quality education, Jean-Baptiste, his father, placed him in the Jesuit College of St Thomas in Rennes in his twelfth year. Louis Marie would not follow his father into business though, his rejection of worldly values meant a commercial career would be a non-starter for him.

As he grew, he continued to spend time alone in prayer rather than playing lads' games with his fellow pupils, and privately he submitted himself to regular mortification from his teenage years (wearing a hair-shirt, and iron armlets under his sleeves). He also prayed daily in his parish church, Saint-Sauveur, to Our Lady, to make him day by day more like her Son. It was during his praying to Our Lady in the Carmelite Church in Rennes that he knew he was being called to serve others as a priest However, though a private boy, he did make some close friends at school, notably Claude Poullart Desplaces, who later founded the Holy Ghost Fathers (1703), and Jean-Baptiste Blain, later Canon of Rouens, who would become his first biographer.[2] Throughout his schooling he proved himself a brilliant student, and when he reached eighteen, expressed a wish to continue his studies in Paris, with a view to entering the seminary of Saint-Sulpice.

### A Seminarian in Paris

When the time came for him to leave home and head for Paris, his parents offered to buy him a horse for the journey but he refused, setting out on foot to travel 230 miles! More than this, his new clothes and money for the

[2] Another biography, also shortly after St Louis Marie's death, was by Joseph Grandet.

journey he gave away to the poor he met *en route*, wearing their clothes in exchange. It was at this time, now reduced to begging himself, to get to Paris, that he made a solemn vow of poverty. His sole possessions were a crucifix and a rosary, and though some biographers have speculated that he also stripped himself of his full name on this journey, he continued to sign himself 'Louis Marie Grignion', though he would refer to himself as *'le Père de Montfort.'*

There was to be disappointment at first in Paris, as a benefactor's promise to secure a place at Saint-Sulpice did not materialise. So he ended up in a small home for poor ecclesiastics. It was here that he met an important influence, M. de la Barmondiere, a pious priest of much experience, who ran the home. Even so, Louis had to contribute to his upkeep in a testing way; keeping watch through the night in the unhealthy environment of the recently dead awaiting burial. But he welcomed this as an opportunity for mortification, humiliation, meditation and prayer. Moreover, there was much he would learn from being in such a macabre setting. This would serve in his later preaching on the horrors of death for he would be able to speak from first-hand experience, not least when a corpse brought in had been in life one of the most beautiful women of the court circle of Louis XIV. Within twenty-four hours he witnessed how hideously changed such beauty could become.

He spent two years in this community before finally being accepted at Saint-Sulpice in 1695, where he would come under the guidance of another major influence (1697), though a hard taskmaster, M. Leschassier, later Superior-General. For the first two years his spiritual director was the more understanding M. Bouin. Here he studied for five years before being ordained in 1700. This was a period that has been described as 'five years hidden with Christ in God', a manifestation of that passage in the First Book of Peter of what is "hidden in a person's heart, in the incorruptibility of a quiet and meek spirit, which is rich in the sight of God." And sometime during 1696-1697, he made his solemn Consecration to Jesus in Mary. This consecration he renewed when chosen, of one of only two students each year, to make a pilgrimage to Our Lady of Chartres in the name of the Saint-Sulpice community, a pilgrimage begun by the seminary's founder, M. Olier. He was delighted to be chosen, for all that was concerned with the honour of Mary was dear to him. Returning from Chartres, he felt he now belonged to Mary. He was all hers (*'totus tuus'*). As he wrote poetically: *"Tout par-elle! Rien sans elle! C'est mon secret pour être parfait."*

Nonetheless, Louis did not spend five years growing in holiness totally apart from the outside world. Of numerous accounts of various instructive occurrences from fellow students and tutors, there was an occasion when he came across two young men fighting a duel. Stepping between their swords with a crucifix and words of prudence and love, he managed to soften their hearts and have them be reconciled with each other. One of the combatants was so impressed he lost interest in the life he was leading, and shortly afterwards was accepted at the seminary to train as a priest

Père Bernard, who would become the fourth Superior of the Order of the Company of Mary, revealed "it was by constant meditation and prayer, and by the practice in a hidden way of humility, obedience, mortification, detachment and love of the poor, interrupted only by his zeal for God's glory, which moved him from time to time to show his contempt for the world by condemning its maxims and practices, that Louis Marie de Montfort endeavoured during the five years he spent at Saint-Sulpice to grow strong in the pure love of God."

We begin to get a picture of one of those rare people who seem literally too good to be true, but true he was, in every sense.

## Ordination

Louis Marie de Montfort was ordained by the Bishop of Perpignan on 5 June 1700. A measure of the extraordinary devoutness of the man was shown by his spending the rest of the day after his ordination in front of the Blessed Sacrament. Then he consecrated several days to preparation for his first Mass, which was in the Lady Chapel of the Church of Saint Sulpice. Burning with a love for God, early on his youthful zeal could have led to impetuosity. He wrote to his spiritual director, declaring "*when I see the needs of the Church, I cannot help pleading continually for a small and poor band of good priests.*" On hearing some new fellow priests were off to Montreal, he spontaneously volunteered to go to Canada, but his offer was refused by M. Leschassier, who was wary of Montfort's level of devotion and, in his eyes, over-zealousness. Instead he was sent to a very poor and holy priest from Nantes, M. Lévêque, and it was in that diocese that he first experienced the influence of the heretical Jansenists in the Church, a group who had become very influential in many parts of France.

On the way to Nantes with the elderly M. Lévêque, who had founded the small community of St Clement there, they made part of their journey by river-boat, from Orleans. On the boat, the rather unworldly Montfort came across three men whose conversation was littered with swearing and blasphemies. He gently admonished them and was met with jeering and ridicule. At which, like a prophet from God, he announced they would soon be punished for their insults to the Lord's name. Within a few days, one died of an excess of alcohol and the others quarrelled and fought, fatally wounding each other.

The eventful journey also saw him take a brief detour to the shrine of Notre Dame des Ardilliers near Saumur. Here he pledged his new life to the patronage of Our Lady of Ardilliers, and the shrine remains very popular today with pilgrims honouring the memory of Montfort. He also visited the Abbey of Fontrevault some nine miles from the shrine to see one of his sisters, soon to be professed as a nun. By November 1700, he was quite established with Fr Lévêque's poor and distracted community at Nantes, where he gave missions with the elderly priest until February 1701.

He seems to have found the little seminary of St Clement worse than he expected. The students had "fallen into a nest of false doctrine and worldliness", he wrote, and the seminary had not "even half the good order of Saint Sulpice." The work he was hoping to do was thwarted by these drawbacks. "I had wished to form myself for the Missions, and in particular for teaching the catechism to the poor, but here I do nothing of that. Few here are fit for such work and there is no-one of experience but M. Lévêque, whose great age means he is no longer able to give missions."

Montfort, nevertheless, always accepted what came to him as God's will. Even so, within himself there was a constant need to be certain that he was doing the right thing (whatever that might be). This would eventually, in 1706, lead to him walking to Rome to go straight to the top, so to speak, to know his purpose for certain through God's Vicar on earth. And, as it happened, he was drawn away from Nantes to Fontrevrault by an invitation from his sister who was now about to become a nun. A little while earlier he had written to another sister, Louise, his favourite, and another religious in this remarkable Grignion family, as she was on the point of being forced to leave the Convent of St Joseph in Paris. The reasons may have been funding, may have been a new policy of only admitting Parisienne girls, but it occasioned a need for him to send words of comfort, and to trust, like himself, in God's will.

At Fontrevarault he met the sister of the Abbess, Madame de Montespan who was impressed with him, despite his shabby appearance. She was a wealthy woman who gave much to charity, and offered to help with funds for his sister's vocation, and to set him up in his own canonry to pursue his missions for the poor. However, generous though this was, he felt this compromised his vow of poverty, but she insisted he at least put her proposal to the Bishop of Poitiers.

### Unexpected Hospital Appointment

Summoned for an interview, he arrived in Poitiers while the Bishop was away and spent the time awaiting his return by helping out at the local hospital. He quickly made an impression and was invited to be the resident priest. The bishop on his return contacted M. Leschassier as to Montfort's suitability. The spiritual director's reply might seem less than kind: "in his outward appearance there is something singular, and his manner and behaviour are not to the taste of many persons, and he has a high idea of perfection, much zeal and little experience. I do not know whether he is fit for the hospital."

The bishop, nonetheless, granted Montfort a trial period as hospital chaplain. The students were much taken with him, and these weeks might be seen as his fruitful entrance into the apostolic life. Even so, he was troubled the while by thoughts of how the infirm M. Lévêque was faring in Nantes. He went back there for a little while, returning to Poitiers with some regret, being on the best of terms with M.Lévêque (who would soon rest in the peace of God). But on his return the post at the hospital was unconditionally offered to him. Once properly in the post, he set about reorganising the treatment of the poor, refused the salary he was entitled to, and the quarters offered him. He insisted on using one of the poorest rooms available, and would only eat what the servants ate.

Despite his good work at Poitiers he met with rebuff and disapproval by some he admired greatly. He continued to keep in touch with and ask guidance from M. Leschassier, who found it an increasing burden having the unique person of Montfort as his penitant. His former superior, M. Brenier, would have nothing to do with him when they met at Saumer in 1702. This was during a break on his way to Paris, where, similarly, the leaders of the seminary at St Sulpice did not welcome back this distinguished son of their community. Though later Sulpicians would rejoice to be associated with the name of Montfort. Perhaps his level of devotion, his intense and constant love of and work for God - God Alone (*'Dieu Seul'*, as he often ended his writings), was overpowering: too much for 'ordinary' religious to emulate. There was joy for him, though, at the end of this visit to Paris, in the witnessing of his sister Louise taking the veil and being admitted among the Dames du Saint-Sacrement.

Back at Poitiers, on top of his labours at the hospital, Montfort resumed his catechism to the local poor, besides preaching in the parish church and giving spiritual direction to the many attracted by his sanctity. His mission work was back in full swing.

## Founding the Daughters of Wisdom

Yet he was not content even with this very full commitment that was his life (a contemporary religious would write that every hour of his day from generally four in the morning to ten-thirty at night would be occupied some way in the work of God). He always wanted to be doing more, to be attracting more souls to God. In effect, seeing the scale of such a goal, he was thinking about some form of delegation. He had already gathered some twenty very poor girls of the hospital into a little company. They helped the similarly poor and the disabled. He gave them the name 'Sagesse', and in 1703 this group became the first of the two Orders he founded, the Order of the Daughters of Wisdom.

Whilst the sisters of *'La Sagesse'* were still an informal community, led by a devout poor woman, herself blind, there came to Fr Montfort for confession a young woman. She would become the first official Superior of the Daughters of Wisdom and the nun who would do so much to guide and establish the Order. Her name was Marie-Louise Trichet. She came, the daughter of a rich local family, to Louis Marie and was surprised when he asked her by whom she had been sent. She replied by her own sister, but Montfort told her this was not so; that the Blessed Virgin herself had directed her. She also confided that she wished one day to be a nun, but wondered whether this would ever happen. He told her with certainty it would, but did not readily give her direction as to how she might proceed. She was only about seventeen at this time, and had expressed an interest in the *La Sagesse* group and their work, but there were no vacancies at the hospital.

She realised her only opportunity to get amongst them (Montfort later revealed he was delighted she had chosen to do this) was to be allowed to be an inmate, to the horror of her parents. Though presumably not to the horror of her brother, for he became a priest and fearlessly served among plague victims, dying young and heroically after contracting the disease. She gained entry and joined the group, among whom she would learn the obedience Montfort knew was absolutely necessary, even for someone he knew was to be exceptional (it is certain he had some prophetic moments, and was graced occasionally to perform the miraculous: the first evidence of this on record was in 1702 when he restored the sight to a poor blind man). In February 1703 she donned a plain habit of cheap grey cloth and began a religious life that would see her become the embodiment of Montfortian spirituality. Though it would be some time before she took her final vows of poverty, obedience and chastity, she would become the first superior of the Daughters of Wisdom, and Catherine Brunet would be her first recruit.

Shortly after this time, and before Miss Trichet would take the name of Sister Marie Louise of Jesus, Montfort's stay at Poitiers came to an abrupt end. He sat down to his meagre supper as usual at the hospital and found a note by his bowl informing him he was dismissed. It is conjectured that others' ambitions and jealousy were the explanation, and there was always in Montfort's life the inability of people around him and his superiors to cope with his saintliness. As it would even more so today, it made people then uncomfortable. Yet, even in this day and age there are, thank God, the Mother Teresa's, the Padre Pio's, the John Paul II's of this world. Montfort always said he welcomed such setbacks, such 'humiliations' as ways of serving God, and even as he received this bolt from the blue, he was informed that one of his sisters, Marie-Catherine, in the novitiate stage at a convent in Rambervilliers, was seriously ill. The timing and the empathy of suffering for Christ could hardly have been more apposite. In love as a 'brother and a priest' he wrote to her: "let your body suffer, but let your heart be firm, for nothing is better for you at the moment than sickness. Pray for ...me. Your brother, Montfort." Of course, then as now, people might well have failed to comprehend how a brother could give such a message to a very sickly sister.

### To Mont-Valerian and Back to Poitiers

His services were not long in being needed elsewhere. On the outskirts of Paris was a brotherhood of hermits at Mont-Valerian, whose superior had been impressed by Montfort since his days as a seminarian in Paris. Abbé Madot invited him to assist at the troubled community, the Archbishop appointing him Visitor Extraordinary. A title truer than perhaps the Archbishop knew!

Again, by his example he gained the admiration of a community that had become fractious, and difficult for

Abbé Madot to direct. He accepted their offer to wear a white habit as theirs, after they had petitioned him so to do, observing him in his threadbare apparel in the cold nights in their hilltop retreat. He also followed their Rule to the letter, an example in itself. Thus he helped very much to turn the community back around, to the Abbé's delight. Meanwhile, the poor of Poitiers, who had nothing to do with his sudden leaving in any sense, petitioned their bishop for Montfort's return. More then this, in 1704, 400 of them signed a similar petition to M. Leschassier, who must have thought he had rid himself of responsibilities over Montfort, who continued to write to him irrespective.

Presumably Lechassier made some gesture, for soon Montfort headed back to Poitiers. About this time further good news for Montfort was a letter that not only had his sister recovered at Rambervilliers, but was now professed as a nun. He wrote to her in celebration: "I deny not that I am a man...it is human, it needs must be, that we yearn towards our dear ones; with delight when they are near, with pain when they are away. I set out immediately for the hospital of Poitiers. I beg of you, my sister, to have no other love than for Jesus alone in Mary, and through Mary for God alone, and in Him alone. Yours devotedly, Montfort."

Re-established at Poitiers, he returned to his tasks and to giving missions in the area. In the town, one day early in 1706, in the Church of the Penitents, he came across a young man from Anjou who had come to Poitiers intending to join the Capuchins. Impressed by his devout saying of the Rosary, Louis Marie approached him, heard his intention and simply said "follow me" The young man, M. Rangeard, at that moment became the first of the Brothers of the Holy Ghost, later to be the Company of Mary. He would become Montfort's constant companion and support in his missions as Brother Mathurin. Though he would remain a lay brother, he would serve the order Montfort founded until 1761.

## Hotfoot to Rome!

In the year of 1706 Montfort felt an irresistible urge to go to Rome to know from the Pope himself, the Lord's true purpose for him. So he set out, on foot all the way, hoping for an audience. He undertook this huge journey without any money and carrying only his religious essentials of a Bible, a breviary, a crucifix, rosary and image of Our Lady. He did get to meet Clement XI on 6 June, who listened patiently to Montfort's desire to leave France to be a missionary in far-off lands, to walk, perhaps, in the steps of St Francis Xavier. Pope Clement's answer was quite clear and unequivocal: "you have in France, Father, a field quite wide enough for the exercise of your zeal. Do not go elsewhere." The Pope bestowed upon him the title of Missionary Apostolic.

Montfort afterwards spoke of experiencing an extraordinary sense of reverence at the sight of the successor of St Peter, as if he had seen Jesus Christ himself in the presence of his Vicar. He left Rome clear now in his head as to the field of his apostolate, and would confine himself to his native north-west of France.

After a period of rest he returned, still managing to fit in two pilgrimages on the way back, to the shrines at Ardilliers and Mont-Saint-Michel. In point of fact, not only these pilgrimages, but he finished off by assisting in a mission taking place at Dinan, and giving one of his own to the soldiers garrisoned at Becherel. At Dinan, he made for the altar of Blessed Alan de la Roche to say Mass. De la Roche, from 1475 also known as 'the darling of the Blessed Virgin' was a fervent promoter of the Rosary, and his altar was in the church of the Dominicans, his order. It was also the order of one of Montfort's brothers, Fr Joseph-Pierre, whom he met up with again after quite some years, and the two brothers worked together in the giving of this mission. Although not before there had been a rather unbrotherly exchange as Joseph felt somewhat slighted by his relatively famous brother not greeting him as 'Father', in recognition that he too was an ordained Grignion!

Intending to progress in this manner, giving missions wherever the opportunity arose, providence again took a hand through the Superior of a community at Saint

Brieuc. Invited to preach there in September 1706, he made a remarkable, one might say destined, contribution to the spiritual uplift of the people at nearby La Cheze. For here was the large but abandoned chapel of Our Lady of Pity. It had no roof and centuries earlier had been observed as abandoned by St Vincent Ferrer. Asked at the time if the chapel might be restored, the saint predicted "this great undertaking was reserved by God for a man ...yet to be born who would be much contradicted and laughed at." Whether or not Montfort was aware of this prophecy, he launched into the task of restoration with great zeal. He found the labourers and skilled artisans required, the task was achieved, and the church became an object for devotion for the local people and many others as the news spread. In gratitude, there was instituted an annual ceremony of cross-bearing and a devotion on the knees around the altar, a little like the devotions at the capelinha chapel in the shrine of Fatima today.

From La Cheze he went to Saint Brieuc to give a retreat to the Daughters of the Cross. In his quiet, but testing way, he did not make any grand plans about his arrival. Instead he sent Brother Mathurin ahead as he neared the convent to beg for alms "for the love of God." He was sent away as the nuns already had sufficient 'deserving poor' to cater for. Shortly after Montfort arrived, declaring who he was and that his assistant had been rebuffed. Apologising profusely the nuns welcomed him and immediately made him a meal. But he had a stern lesson for the nuns, admonishing them for preparing a splendid meal because they knew who he was, but having refused to give "a crust of bread asked of you in the name of Jesus Christ" It was not the first time he had done this, for a few months earlier in November 1706 he had taught a similar lesson to his own foster-mother when he passed through the village where she lived in retirement. He had also sent Br Mathurin ahead that day to beg for alms, which were refused him by the suspicious Mother André. Then finding out who had sent for alms, she begged him to eat with her. He did accept, but told her: "forget about Fr Grignion, he is worthless. Instead, remember Jesus Christ, who is our All, and it is He who is the poor."

He spent much of 1707 continuing his missionary work, before withdrawing into solitude for a while to Saint-Lazare, and then in November giving a mission in Bre'al. Here an incident occurred that almost cost him his life, but yet also demonstrated his profound trust in God and the gift of prophecy clearly granted him at important moments in his earthly ministry. Seeing a man beating his wife in the street Montfort endeavoured to calm the man, but the husband came at him with a hatchet. Montfort knelt to take the blow but the man's hands stiffened at the very point of violence, and the weapon dropped from his hands. Despite this 'lesson', he would not be pacified, at which Montfort told him he would lose his (considerable) wealth, and die a beggar. That this came to pass was later verified by the priest who gave the man the last sacraments, as he lay dying on a bed of straw in a house for the poor. After Bre'al he gave a last mission in Ramille, the last he would give in the diocese of Saint-Malo, where he was not allowed to minister freely and which he left in 1708, never to return.

### Calvary at Pontchateau

He went to the neighbouring diocese of Nantes where he was soon given a mission in Pontchateau. This would result in one of the most extraordinary passages of his life. It was towards the end of July 1709 that he would arrive in this village, and be pleasantly surprised by the scale of devotion already existing there. He was gratefully received by his fellow priest, M. de Bastières, and Montfort felt the time and place right to thank God with a project he had been considering for some while. Probably inspired by the great Calvary in his time at Mont-Valerian overlooking Paris, he announced he wished to build such a monument here, judging the people as worthy and deserving of such a memorial (even though Pontchateau had no real hills to speak of!).

They willingly agreed to help, without perhaps realising the huge scale of the project, to honour Christ

Crucified. When he finally chose the site, several of the older residents came forward to say how they recalled quite some time earlier, quite possibly the date of Montfort's birth, seeing in a clear sky, crosses with banners coming down from the heavens towards the very spot chosen for the calvary. All the local people pitched in along with the craftsmen. The work lasted into 1710, and it was not uncommon to see 400 or 500 labourers engaged in construction, using over 100 carts and oxen, and including wives and daughters helping in the great work. Over 282,000 cubic feet of white clay were dug out to build the hill and the route to the summit. In all the work took fifteen months, and was, by all accounts, a great sight; a wonderful achievement.

But as ever, Montfort had his enemies. It is argued that mainly Jansenist priests sought to have this Calvary taken down even as it was being finished. Petition was made to the bishop who summoned Montfort back from a mission he had left to give only four days earlier. The military were consulted on the grounds that the hill could strategically be used by enemies for a fortress in an attack. To the great dismay of all the local people the order was given for it to be dismantled. Montfort, saddened, but always accepting such 'humiliations' for God, said: "God be blessed. I have not sought my own glory but His. I hope to receive the same reward as if I had succeeded." He went straight way to make a retreat with the Jesuit fathers in Nantes. But the Pontchateau Calvary would not be forgotten, indeed its remnants became a place of devotion for many years before a new and later a third lasting Calvary was built in the 19th century.

## Becomes a Dominican Tertiary

He stayed some time in the city of Nantes, not giving any missions but intensifying his prayerful contemplations and probably applying himself to some of his main writings. His great devotion to Our Blessed Lady led to his wish to show his high regard for the great saint with which the giving of the Rosary is associated. He expressed a wish to join the Third Order of St Dominic (also known at the time as the Third Order of Penance), and was professed as a Dominican tertiary on 10 November, 1710 in the Convent of the Dominicans at Nantes. About this time, a pious lady gave him a small house in which he fitted a little chapel, and was allowed to say Mass. Soon after he acquired a similar property close by to serve as a refuge for the incurable poor. In effect thereby, he founded Nantes' first 'hospice'. Nor was that all he did for the poor of that city. There came some days of serious flooding, and a community of poor people became stranded on a little Loire islet. starvation was as much a threat to their lives as drowning. But the waters were felt too dangerous for any rescue craft. Somehow, Montfort persuaded some boatmen to risk it, himself acting as pilot. Food was got to the people, who survived, as did the boat crews.

## Poison and Pirates

At last, he was given another mission, this time in La Rochelle, for which he left in March, 1711, first giving a retreat in the Lucon diocese and making a retreat with some Capuchin fathers. Paying his respects to the Bishop of Lucon before continuing to La Rochelle, he was reciprocally invited to preach in the cathedral. Turning to a discourse on the Rosary, he referred to St Dominic's problem with re-converting the Albigensians. Montfort found out later that the bishop, who was most understanding, himself came from Albi (indeed, research by Fr Simon Tugwell, OP, suggests that despite giving its name to the notorious heresy, the town of Albi was not the seedbed for apostates that one would infer). However, just like St Dominic, Montfort would come face-to-face with the problem of heretics in France, this time of a Calvinist nature.

Though he met with success in numerous and significant conversions, not least of a prominent townswoman and vociferous heretic, Madame de Mailly, and though he even moved the soldiers of the La Rochelle garrison to tears with his preaching, he was the victim of an attack in the form of the poisoning of his broth one evening. He did recover, but he was seriously weakened, for he had been a man of considerable strength when he wished to use it, in physical labour or in carrying a sick tramp to a place of refuge.

Still he continued his work, accepting, in February 1712, an appointment to preach on the island of Ile-Dieu. After being nearly poisoned to death, his short sea-journey met with attack by pirates, corsairs operating out of Guernsey, probably in the pay of the Calvinists, irked by his missionary successes. Surviving yet again, he was welcomed by the islanders and the resident priest, M. Heron. He stayed two months, and a memento of his visit there is preserved with the Montfort fathers at St Laurent-sur-Sevres. It is a panel from the door of the room where he stayed, on which he had carved the initials 'IHS'.

Back on the mainland he continued giving missions, achieving further conversions, countering the work of the devil, which he would see not only in some great evil deed as ordinary people would recognise, but in the way people behaved or misused their talents. A notable example of the latter occurred when a pretty, well-to-do, frivolous and witty young woman turned up at the front for one of his sermons to catch him out for the amusement of her friends. After Montfort finished, however, her friends could not budge her and she remained for two hours in conversation with the remarkable priest. The very next morning, without disclosing her plans to family or friends, she packed some things, left her home, and became a cloistered religious with the nuns of St Clare for the remaining thirty years of her life.

### Hermitage of Saint Eloi

He was content to stay and work in La Rochelle the rest of the year and into 1713, during which time a benefactor gave him a small house which he called his Hermitage of Saint-Eloi, after the district in which it was situated. The artist in him was quickly at work, and after hollowing out a niche in the chimney, he carved a Christ and several other figures to place there. The hollow would become a place of great reverence for generations to come. After the succession of setbacks and diabolical attacks he had experienced throughout his life, he now found he met with little opposition. He was, in fact, able to write to his sister in her Order of Perpetual Adoration at Rambervilliers in January 1713: "God takes pleasure, dear Sister, in seeing us combat for Him, and in making both of us victorious; you in secret, and your brother in public. Your combats take place in yourself, they are not seen out of your community, but mine are seen throughout the whole of France, whether in struggling with the devils of hell, or in making war against the world and the worldly enemies of all truths."

## Founding the Company of Mary

Although he had set up his first Order in 1703 (The Daughters of Wisdom), and at a local level had set up small Associations, such as The Daughters of the Cross, The Company of Virgins, The White Penitents, The Friends of the Cross, and The Soldiers of St Michael, he had not yet established a community of priests. There was a general community of followers composed of priests and lay brothers, but they were not an order whose fathers would consecrate their lives to carry on his work after his death. That work would be to further and continue the fruitful labour of his missions, according to his method. This intention and its details he passed on to the Bishop of La Rochelle, who was supportive. Initially such priests as he found would operate under the title of The Congregation of The Holy Ghost. But finding them was not straightforward, and he went to Paris to seek assistance especially at a small seminary founded by a friend from his early days, Abbé Desplaces. This friend had died four years earlier, but Montfort found in his successor at the Saint-Esprit community an admirer of his work, M. Bovic.

Here he met "young ecclesiastics who had a vocation for the missions of the Company of Mary." Unfortunately, as they were not yet sufficiently trained and the community being quite small, Abbé Bovic did not feel he could lose even one of his charges, just yet. However, he pledged to help Montfort in any way he could, when he could. Montfort understood, and he had come up with the title of his Order during his stay at Saint Esprit. Just as he had reinforced to all the importance of the Rosary with his words there in one of his seminars: *let me put my Rosary around a sinner's neck and he shall not escape me.* Soon young priests from Saint-Esprit would be allowed to join the Company of Mary at its future home in Saint-Laurent-sur-Sevres. Montfort had, at least in principle, founded his order of priests. An interesting account of the vocation of one of those first young priests to make the journey to join the Montfort fathers is given to us by Père Caris, who almost joined Montfort when he left Saint Esprit, but who was too much needed by the seminary. There was a student of questionable calling who one day went into his tutor's room and ripped up all the holy pictures therein, including one of Montfort. He then went, grinning, to the priest, Fr Le Valois, to say he would find quite a surprise when he returned to the room. He did. The picture of Montfort was entirely whole, with only faint marks to show where it had been ripped. The foolish young man was cured of his mental problems and became a devout Montfortian.

After leaving Saint-Esprit, he took a much-needed vacation, before heading for his next mission near to La

Rochelle. Here he gladly accepted the offer of assistance from two Jesuits, one of whom, Père Coulsson, was a celebrated Professor of Theology. Their help was perhaps divinely sent, as Montfort became so ill by the end of the mission, early in 1714, that he had to be taken to hospital.

### New Role for Sr Marie-Louise of La Sagesse

Even as a temporary invalid, he was able to communicate to the Bishop of La Rochelle his vision for a girls school, and that it should be put under the charge of Sr Marie-Louise of Jesus. With the Bishop's approval, Montfort wrote to the co-founder of the Daughters of Wisdom, saying she was to leave Poitiers in six months time, and undertake a new educational duty. Leaving was not an easy thing for the young nun, as she was well aware there was the question of who would organise hospital affairs once she had gone. It also meant she would be out of arm's reach of her mother, Madame Trichet, who had never approved of her joining Montfort's Order. Her father was much more understanding and helped arrange transport for his daughter and her companion, Sr de la Conception. They reached La Rochelle in March 1715.

During this time, Montfort was back on his feet, though much weakened, and he had set off for Rouen. He left a message for Sr Marie-Louise should she arrive before his return, telling her to call her group the "Community of Wisdom for the instruction of children and the care of the poor." In this time also he acquired his first priest for the Company of Mary, M.Vatel. Together they gave the first mission of this priestly order at Taugon-la-Ronde, followed by another success at Saint-Arnand. In between he snatched time to pay a visit to Sr Marie-Louise of Jesus, and gave her a list of directions to be the Rule of her order. She went to her knees in accepting this, as if it was the most wonderful gift imaginable.

## Enlists his Successor

He returned once more to his life's work of presenting missions, this time at Fontenay in August 1715. It was here that the vocation of M. Mulot occurred, a calling of great importance as this priest, on Montfort's death, became the Superior-General of the Company of Mary. He had also been in poor health, and was staying with his brother, the curé of the parish. He was inspired by Montfort and offered his services, which were not immediately accepted. This would seem to be consistent with Montfort's way of ensuring his followers, the followers of Jesus through Mary, were certain and sincere. Pressed again by M. Mulot, he acceded: "well, then, promise to labour with me for the rest of your life." He then set him the task of joining him in his next mission at Vouvant. Thus arrived the second priest of the Company of Mary.

## Last Pilgrimage

Early in January 1716, perhaps foreseeing the approach of death, he organised a pilgrimage to Notre Dame des Ardilliers, taking thirty-three members of an association, the Confraternity of Penitents, and placing himself a little way behind the party. Fathers Vatel and Mulot were placed at the front. He wanted to ensure that nothing of a Chaucerian Tale nature was to take place. More than this, he wrote out fifteen conditions to be observed by the priests, as they set the example, during the days of the walk. It is hard to imagine any but the most exceptional of religious following all his conditions today, changed times notwithstanding. Some examples taken from these instructions are as follows:

(1) you will have no other object in this pilgrimage but to obtain of God, through the intercession of the Blessed Virgin, good missionaries for His people, who may walk in the footsteps of the apostles.

(2) you will not be distinguished from others by your dress, but by a great modesty, religious silence, and continual prayer during the course of your journey;

(5,i) the pilgrims will all go to bed, if possible, in the same inn, the more penitential on hay and straw, and the weak on beds.

(5,ii) they will rise at daybreak and recite a short prayer, together with the commandments of God and the Church (and if church is nearby, obtain Exposition of the Blessed Sacrament and sing the *Tantum Ergo*, followed by prayers).

(5,viii) at the inn, if possible, before eating they will go to an upper room, kneel down and sing the *Veni Sancte Spiritu*, and one *Ave Maria*.

(8) A quarter of an hour before entering the town of the shrine, they may take off their shoes and enter two by two, singing hymns.

(15) on their return, they will give an account of all the crosses which they had to bear, and of the principal things which have happened to them.

Arduous though this was, the Rule was observed. Montfort, though exhausted, and near his last days, could be pleased. Even so, still no rest as he went to St Laurent-sur-Sevres to give a mission on 1 April 1716, as ever requesting only straw for his bed. M. Mulot came to see him, M. Vatel had work elsewhere. Towards the end of the month on the 27 April, Montfort made his will, beginning: "I, the undersigned, the greatest of sinners, desire that my body be placed in the cemetery and my heart under the pavement of the altar of the Blessed Virgin" (In the event, he was buried 'entire' under Our Lady's altar at St Laurent-sur-Sevre). The following day, weak and confined to bed, he suddenly shouted out in the evening, defying the devil to the last, "it is in vain that you attack me. I am between Jesus and Mary.....it is over now, and I shall never sin again." A little later, at 8 o'clock on the 28 April 1716, he died.

## Reflection on His Life

What do you say about a man like St Louis-Marie de Montfort? Surely the word 'superhuman' is not out of place. In his physical trials that he imposed on himself everyday, in his work, in his fasting, in his self-denial, in his mortifications, he undertook much more than any reasonable human being could ask, or could emulate. In the devotion he had and the divine assistance he clearly was given at times, he was more than human in his spirituality, compared to most people's spiritual gifts. Or was it that the level of his devotion, of his constant prayer, of his constant searching for truth and the path to Jesus, the Eternal Wisdom, through a colossal love for Our Blessed Lady, elevated this man to the saint-on-earth that he was?

Is it excusable, or just an excuse, to say that this was all 300 years ago? Things are so different now, times so changed, the world an altered place, so how could anyone be expected to be his sort of saint. And the Church tut-tuts or downrightly forbids where mortifying the flesh is concerned, while 'sacrifice' is hardly ever spoken of as part of a Catholic's devotion to Christ. Yet we probably know there is quite a difference between what ostensibly seems masochistic, and what is an expression of deep love for Christ and great sorrow for sin, for what sin has done (if a visual lesson is needed here, Mel Gibson's *The Passion Of The Christ* is painfully true and devout). Yes, the world has changed, but what has time to do with an immortal soul that is the gift of God, that is the spiritual temple of pure, innocent love. The potential loss of which in others drives all our known and unknown saints in this life, whenever they lived and shall live, whatever the primitive or technologically-advanced times they might be born into. The temptations may be much greater and more all around us now, but it is still as it always has been since the Incarnation, whether a person accepts or rejects that Christ is the Way, the Truth and the Life.

Louis Marie de Montfort strove all his life for the saving of souls, for the guiding of souls to Jesus, through Mary. His like, in different ways, has been seen in every generation, even yet in our own increasingly secular and spiritually threatened world. In offering some examples, one is not singling out members, worldwide, of *the Church militant, suffering or (sic) triumphant,* but the likes of Mother Teresa of Calcutta, Josemaria Escriva, Maximillian Kolbe, Oscar Romero, Sister Faustina and John Paul II spring to mind. In his time, Louis Marie de Montfort was also vilified for his 'oddball' behaviour, as devout religious in our day and age are. He persevered, he led by example, and obviously not an example for most people to be called upon to follow. He trusted in God, God alone, and the path to Jesus through Mary, which we can all try to emulate.

## His Writings

Throughout his missionary work, incredibly busy though he always was, he kept up his private writings, from *cantiques* and poetry to devotional tracts and sermons. In doing this, he was effectively putting together those books which are unsurpassed in the understanding of the role of Mary in the Rosary, and the purpose of the Rosary itself. In a nutshell it is *'ad Jesum per Mariam'*, to Jesus through Mary. This is the underlying theme and teaching of *'The Secret of the Rosary'*, *'The Secret of Mary'*, and *'True Devotion to Mary'*, all stemming from his initial work *'The Eternal Wisdom'*. *'The Secret of the Rosary'*, a slim volume, has become a very popular paperback over the last forty-five years, and has currently sold over 5.4 million copies through thirty printings. It has a commentary for every single 'rose' of each decade. *'True Devotion'*, of which *'The Secret of Mary'* is a shortened version, is profound and needs to be read several times, as Pope John Paul II himself has said. It is an important, reflective guide that Montfort predicted would be lost for many years, but would be found for later generations. This proved to be true. For after having been hidden from the manic destruction of the mobs of the French Revolution, it was found, by chance, in an old chest in 1842, by one of the Montfort Fathers of the Company of Mary, in their community at St Laurent-sur-Sevre.

### The Eternal Wisdom

Written around 1703 or 1704, this was Louis Marie's first book, and it was probably written for students at the senior seminary of the Holy Ghost Fathers recently founded by his school friend Poullart Desplaces. It is "a very important book, which places his devotion to Mary in its proper context of commitment to Jesus Christ" (Fr Paul Allerton SMM). Montfort refers to Jesus Christ as 'Eternal Wisdom', the eternal and incarnate Wisdom who is "an infinite treasure for man." He declares, in passages 64 and 66 of the book, that the bond of friendship between the eternal Wisdom and man is so close as to be beyond our understanding. Wisdom is for man and man is for Wisdom. Since Wisdom, out of an excess of love, gave Himself up to death to save man, He loves man as a brother, a friend, a disciple, a pupil, the price of His own blood and the co-heir of His kingdom. For man to withhold his heart from Wisdom or to wrench it away from Him would constitute an outrage. As Montfort puts it, in every public place, anywhere, Wisdom proclaims *"listen, draw close to Me. For I want to make you happy."*

Most of the book is about showing the love of Wisdom throughout history, especially in the mysteries of the Incarnation and the Cross.

## True Devotion to Mary

(*The Treatise on the True Devotion to the Blessed Virgin*) One can summarise this not-at-all-straightforward devotion as being wholly about understanding that the most perfect path to reaching Jesus, to being one with Him, is through His mother: *Ad Jesum per Mariam*. It is how a person reaches Wisdom: through a genuine and loving devotion to the Blessed Virgin. Montfort teaches that our whole Christian life consists in welcoming Jesus who comes to share with us the love of His Father. Each day is as at the first Christmas: Jesus 'comes' to us through Mary (passages 1,13,22 *et al*).

He goes on to show how if Mary was necessary to God, who accepted He could depend on Mary, as it were, how much more is she necessary to us, and how much we should depend upon her. We as her children can depend on Mary, our mother. The perfect devotion to the Blessed Virgin consists in consecrating oneself to Jesus through her and practising this consecration in everyday life by doing everything through, with, in, and for Mary in order to be more closely united to Jesus.

In 273 passages, St Louis Marie leads us toward a formal Act of Consecration to Jesus in this way. He also recommends in a supplement at the end of his treatise that one might take up to three weeks undergoing exercises in preparation for this Consecration.

### The Secret of Mary

This is in effect a summary of the book above, *True Devotion*. It proposes the same form of devotion to Mary on the potential, or rather intention of our vocation to holiness. The means to become saints are varied, understood and known, but far from easy. Certainly it is absolutely necessary to obtain the grace from God that comes from following in their footsteps. In order to obtain this grace we need Mary. This is a "secret" that only the Holy Spirit can reveal.

### The Secret of the Rosary

This much-loved little book of Montfort's guide to saying the Rosary has sold over 5 million copies in paperback since the 1960's, and is in its thirtieth edition. St Louis Marie describes each 'Hail Mary' as a 'rose', and has a contemplation for each 'rose' of each decade, which can be applied to any of the Mysteries, as they are simply numbered (one to fifty). He does propose short prayers as offerings before each decade of the original three Mysteries. Early in the devotion he recognises the debt to St Dominic for the gift of the Rosary ('third rose'), and to another Dominican, Blessed Alan de la Roche ('fourth rose'). Blessed Alan, 200 years later, revived and promoted the saying of the Rosary at a time in which this devotion to Our Lady was in serious decline. A noted writer of the Order of Preachers, Fr R. Poupon, writing of Louis Marie's contribution to the Rosary, states: "Montfort's genius prolongs in one straight line that of Blessed Alan de la Roche and of St Dominic. He completes them by bringing forth a personal grace and interpretation." The contemplations are varied in their focus, including an *Explanation of the Hail Mary* (20th. Rose[3]), *Blanche of Castille, Queen of France* (31st), *Fighting Distractions* (43rd.), and *Group Recitiation* (46th.)

## The Letter to the Friends of the Cross

This is another little book, smaller and of much less scope. Nonetheless it is an important short guide to acquiring Wisdom. It advocates universal mortification on the basis of Jesus' own teachings in the Gospels. Montfort breaks down the words of Christ for those who would become His disciples into four steps or

---

[3] At the end of this contemplation, Montfort writes: *"at the end of each decade it is very good to add a Gloria Patri."* So it is very probable that the saying of the *'Glory be to the Father'* as a seemingly natural part of the Rosary, is actually an addition attributable to St Louis Marie himself. Just as the Mysteries of Light three hundred years later are a Marian gift through Pope John Paul II, and the addition after the 'Glory be' of the prayer *'O Jesus, save us from the fires of hell, lead all souls to Heaven, especially those most in need of Thy mercy'*, is a recommendation by Our Lady herself at Fatima in 1917.

stages: (1) *if anyone wants to follow Me* (2) *let him renounce himself* (3) *let him take up his cross* (4) *let him follow Me*. Each of these steps Montfort elaborates upon as a means of acquiring Wisdom.

## Prayer for Missionaries

This is a moving prayer and powerful rallying-cry asking God for missionaries. Fr L. Le Crom, a biographer of Montfort, states it is so impressive that such a cry is "seldom heard issuing from human lips with such magnificent power". Fr Faber (First Provost of London Oratory, writer of *Faith of Our Fathers*), the translator of Montfort's *True Devotion*, also said of this *Prayer*: "since the Epistles written by the Apostles, it would be difficult to find words so ardent."

## Other Works

He also wrote song-poems or 'cantiques' from an early age, as well as numerous pamphlets and hymns. In fact he wrote 164 hymns for his missions, some of them being of considerable length. One dedicated priest of the Company of Mary, Fr Jean Morinay, has painstakingly counted that the total number of lines of all the poems added together is some 23,000! The hymns would be set to popular tunes and sung during the cermonies. He consciously took up his pen to record his teachings for the benefit of all he would meet and give missions to. In so doing he gave posterity the ingredients of Montfortian spirituality, of the message reawakening in the present world that the way to Jesus is through Mary. All his writing, 'the complete works' is substantial, but with typical humility his comment on this monumental achievement was "*all my trouble will have been worthwhile if this little writing should fall into the hands of a spiritual soul.*"

Outside of writing and preaching, he would put much personal effort into his promotion of the Love of Jesus, including organising the restoration of a number of churches. Moreover he had no little skill as an artist and carver, producing many images of Our Lady and Jesus from adornments of walking-sticks to personal gifts and statues for the churches.

## His Canonisation

### The English Miracle

To become a saint in the Catholic Church, two proven miracles attributable to the direct intercession of the saint are necessary. An unusual aspect of the Montfort canonisation is that one of the miracles involved a young English woman. Though she came from one of the traditional Catholic counties, Lancashire, her country at the time very much saw itself as being Protestant. Recorded miracles in England in the last three hundred years are very rare indeed.

The miracle occurred on the 8 April 1927. The young woman was Sister Gerard du Calvaire, born Margaret Cottom, in a village near Chorley in 1898. She was a teenage convert to the Faith, and had been professed as a Sister of La Sagesse only two-and-a-half years previously, and even as a postulant had shown signs of illness. In the Abbey House at Romsey, Hampshire, where she helped in the Orphanage, this illness gradually became serious. She had tuberculosis. Despite surgery, she deteriorated, and though a fighter, was compelled to bed with a permanent watch upon her from 31 March 1927.

Three days later she received the Last Sacraments. Expecting her death imminently, a Sister gave her a relic of St Pius X. Shortly after she had a dream in which St Louis Marie de Montfort appeared, saying he would intercede to prevent her immediate death. On waking Sr Gerard announced that if she was to be saved it would be through the intercession of her Order's founder, not the good pope. However, on the 7 April she slipped in and out of consciousness regularly as the Sisters continued a special novena to St Louis Marie. On 8 April, Sr Gerard was prepared for her final vows, also sending for a relic of St Louis Marie. For three days the young nun had been unable to swallow even water and there was a terrible stench from an abdomen wound. Then, for a brief moment that she was alone, clutching the relic of Montfort as her pains worsened, she saw a cloud of incense in which, very clearly, was the figure of Our Lady. To the side was the long-haired (auburn and not black as usually depicted) figure of St Louis Marie in the habit of a Montfort Missionary. She asked for his blessing and crossed herself with the relic. When she woke she was fully recovered, her swollen abdomen normal, and where she had seen Our Lady at the foot of the bed there were just the traces of a small cloud.

On 11 April the local doctor arrived with a death certificate expecting Sr Gerard to be with God by now. He found her cheerfully sweeping and polishing the large main corridor! The miracle was reported in '*The Universe*' of 8 July 1927: " nun at death's door cured suddenly - intercession of Blessed de Montfort, Founder of her Community."

The process of the verification of the miracle by the Church took some time, but backed by a subsequent miracle (the cure of a dying French nun in 1934), the canonisation of Blessed Louis Marie de Grignion Montfort by Pope Pius XII took place on 20 July 1947. In his canonisation address, the pope declared "the greatest force behind all his apostolic ministry and his secret for attracting and winning souls for Jesus was his devotion to Mary."

## His Legacy

### Daughters of Wisdom (Sisters of La Sagesse)

In 1703 Montfort founded the Daughters of Wisdom, while based at a hospital in Poitiers. He was inspired by meeting a seventeen year old young woman who would become foundress of the Order with him. She was Marie-Louise Trichet who came to see him. Asked who had sent her, she replied it was her sister.

But he said "no!...it was the Blessed Virgin herself." She would have to undergo a ten-year preparation before Louis Marie would give her the habit of the congregation, but she persevered, became the Superior and stuck to the initial purpose of the founding: *to instruct children in charitable schools...take good care of the poor, whether in hospitals or not, sick or not, incurable or not, and conduct retreat houses*. When she died in 1759 it was on exactly the same day as Montfort had died, 28 April, in the same village, Saint-Laurent-sur-Mer, at the same hour. Her memorial is next to St Louis Marie's on the altar by his tomb there. When she died there were 150 Sisters of La Sagesse. Now, worldwide, there are over 4,000. Ironically, the French Revolution of 1789 which so persecuted religious communities led to the Sisters beginning a 'wandering life', thirty-three sisters giving their lives during the revolutionary purges. In 1811 the restored French state under Napoleon I legally approved the work of the Daughters of Wisdom, since which time the sisters have committed themselves worldwide, in hospitals, schools and prisons to the needs of the blind, deaf-mutes, children, prisoners and the poor in general.

### Company of Mary (Montfort Missionaries)

In his numerous missions, Montfort often sought to leave some memorial or create some institution to preserve the fruits of a mission. It might be the erection of a calvary, the decoration of a chapel or the formation of an association, usually small and local, such as the 'White Penitents', the 'Friends of the Cross' or the 'Soldiers of St Michael'. He also had a wish to create two much larger institutions. This he achieved in part in 1703 with the setting up of the Order of the Daughters of Wisdom. He also wanted to commence a Company of Priests to carry on the work, after his death, that he had started: to consecrate their lives to the fruitful labour of the missions. So busy was virtually every day of his life that it was not until during a vacation in 1713 that he got round to this project. He travelled to the community of Saint-Esprit in Paris to find recruits, a community founded less than a decade before by a fellow Breton, M. Desplaces. He had died in 1709, but his successor, Abbé

Bovic, was as helpful as he could be. The seminarians were young, of course, but many would tread the miles to Saint Laurent-sur-Sevres soon after Montfort's death to join the Company of Mary (sometimes also referred to by Montfort as the Congregation of the Holy Ghost) where the Order set up its first main base.

Though the Order grew, up until the late 1800's the Company of Mary confined itself to the north-western area of France. Perhaps it was echoing Montfort's own obedient response to the direction of Pope Clement XI in 1706 to their founder. In 1871 this changed with a mission to Haiti. Then persecution by the French government led to a spread of the congregation to Canada, Belgium, the Netherlands and England. This dispersion has continued and today the Montfort Missionaries are found in over thirty countries across the globe. The building up of young churches and the spreading of the sprituality of St Louis Marie de Montfort are top of the agenda priorities. Also high on the agenda is the 'new evangelisation' called for by Pope John Paul II, surely destined to be one of the great Marian popes. There is considerable success in this evangelisation where poorer countries are concerned (contrasted with the 'western' ones) with new vocations in such places as Indonesia, the Philippines, India, Haiti, Colombia, Peru and in several African countries.

The first members of the Company of Mary in England arrived in 1891, with the priest who came to be chaplain to the Sisters of La Sagesse at Romsey (where the 'English Miracle' in Montfort's canonisation occurred). A larger group arrived in 1910. A Junior Seminary was built nearby, initially for boys from France, but a little later it also accepted English boys. Ramifications of World War II led to some changes of the siting of seminaries including in Lancashire and Shropshire, and Totton, Hants where the English Province (now Gt. Britain and Ireland) was inaugurated. In 1948 a Mission House was established in Liverpool, followed by one in Leeds, and from these centres teams of missionaries went out to many parts of the UK. In 1961 the first Mission houses were set up in Scotland and Ireland. These Missionary Montfortians also gave retreats, in the main to Religious Congregations.

Another main task for the SMM priests has been to spread the teachings of St Louis Marie himself, particularly regarding "the perfect devotion to Mary", which is to say *Total Consecration to Jesus through the hands of Mary*. From the Liverpool base a magazine promoting such teaching was published for many years, entitled '*Queen and Mother*'. This ended through financial pressures in the 1970's but a small revival through the newsletter '*In the Footsteps of St Louis Marie de Montfort*' continues to promote the teachings. The

Montfort Press has also been set up to disseminate St Louis Marie's teachings in English, and to promote books concerning his teachings. The Confraternity, now known as *The Association of Mary Queen of All Hearts*, was also established to support those who follow the devotion of the Saint.

In recent years there have been changes in the use of some of the Mission Houses, particularly after the decline in the demand for parish missions following Vatican II. The reduction in the number of personnel to run the centres has meant that only Barrhead in Scotland operates as a retreat house. The centre in Liverpool is run by lay people, while the one at Totton has been converted to a reception centre for refugees and asylum seekers. On the more positive side, provided a parish has a certain 'missionary' flavour, a need for true renewal or a deepening of spiritual life, the Company of Mary now takes on the care of such parishes for a limited period. Parish missions also continue, albeit with a reduced team. When there were members who could be spared in the 1980s and 1990s, SMMs went out on the 'foreign missions' from the UK (particular to Malawi and Uganda, and on a temporary basis to India and the Philippines), though that was not originally the charism of the Montfort Missionaries in the UK.

However, the key point was and is the undertaking of being 'missionaries of the Company of Mary', to preach the message of the Gospel to those most in need, always inspired by and in company with Mary, the Mother of God and our Mother.

## Brothers of St Gabriel

The Brothers can trace their roots back to a boys' school in La Rochelle in 1714, for which St Louis Marie expressly wished to have appropriate Masters put in charge. It was some time later, in 1835, the Brothers became a formal body in their present name, with their own house, and their own first Superior-General. This was M. Gabriel Deshayes, effectively their Founder in 1823, and after whom they are named. But their Rule of Life has always been Montfortian, e.g in the 'consecration of the world', the 'knowledge of Christ Wisdom' and the 'loving relationship with Mary'.

They first came to England in 1903, and, unusually, until 1968 all the Brothers lived together under one roof in a series of successive addresses throughout the country, starting in Plymouth. In the early days, the brothers would mostly come from France, and after training and work in England head off for missionary points in Asia and Africa. There had been a request for help from the St Gabriel Brothers by a priest in Sussex in 1875, but it was not until the hostile French government forced the Brothers abroad in 1903, that their work began this side of the Channel. From the earliest days they provided for poor and disabled boys, particularly the deaf, moving on to London in 1906 and a number of different houses: in Stockwell, in Clapham, and near Wimbledon (Oaklands) until 1968. After this there was dispersal for the first time, and also some working in education institutions run by bodies other than the S.G.s themselves, such as in Welwyn Garden City and at Feltham Young Offenders Prison. The Brothers are now based at Southall and Ealing.

Whilst there has been a reduction in numbers and vocations in England and Europe in recent years, vocations have increased in the poorer continents. There are thriving centres of learning run by the Brothers in, for example, Madras, Thailand, Singapore, Madagascar, Senegal, Congo and Brazil. In fact, statistically, the Brothers of St Gabriel are to be found in Canada, USA, eight of the Latin Americas, twelve European countries, eighteen African countries and nine in Asia. In all these places, in the steps of St Louis Marie de Montfort, the Brothers dedicate their lives to helping children, young people, adults, deaf or blind people and the poor in the field of education.

## Legion Of Mary

All the members of the Legion of Mary, and there are 16 dioceses with branches in England alone, have a strong connection with St Louis Marie de Montfort. For the

Residents at Oaklands during the first year of Saint Gabriel's College (1949-1950)

Saint is their patron. The spreading of Montfortian spirtuality had developed in the British Isles with the arrival of the La Sagesse Sisters, the Company of Mary and the Brothers of St Gabriel. But it had begun earlier through the parish priests of Lancashire. For the then Bishop Vaughan of Salford (later Cardinal) after reading Fr Faber's[4] translation of Montfort's *Treatise on the True Devotion to the Blessed Virgin* (1862), recommended the reading of the '*True Devotion*' to all the priests in his diocese. It was also taken up in English seminaries, and thereby, in some measure, would be spread in other dioceses. Of course, most of this promotion of Montfortian devotion was by 'religious', but from 1921 a considerable number of ordinary lay women would be part of the spreading of Montfort's message. For this was when Frank Duff, who was a great devotee of Bl. Louis Marie (as he was then), founded the Legion of Mary, in Dublin. It soon came to be said that the spirit of the Legion of Mary was the spirit of Montfort applied to Catholic action.

## Dominican Nuns of the Perpetual Rosary

Some forty-four years before the birth of St Louis Marie, in 1629, the people of Italy were facing the ravages of the plague. With no means of control the plague claimed

[4] Fr Frederick William Faber, founder of the London Oratory and writer of such classic hymns as *Faith Of Our Fathers and O Purest Of Creatures*.

more and more lives. During this desperate time, which also witnessed much moral decay, a Dominican priest, Fr. Timothy Ricci, had been preaching the Rosary throughout Italy, and had seen numerous miracles and favours obtained through the fervent recitation of this prayer. He was inspired by what he saw to organise the perpetual recitation of the Rosary by the people in their homes, where many were confined to contain the spread of disease. Each person would agree to pray one hour. Soon, Fr Ricci had enough people 'signed up' to ensure that each hour of the day there was someone praying the Rosary. This blossomed throughout the major cities of Italy, and thus the Perpetual Rosary was born. Later an Association (1635) was formed and approved by the Church. The Dominican Order in keeping with the Rosary tradition of St Dominic (and which Order Louis Marie de Montfort joined as a Tertiary in 1710), has been the custodian of this Association from the start. Anybody may join this Association, committing themselves to an 'Hour of Guard' per month saying the Rosary.

After preaching and organising the Perpetual Rosary for some years, Fr Damien Marie Saintourens, OP., founded the Dominican Nuns of the Perpetual Rosary, whose Motherhouse is in Fatima. These cloistered, contemplative nuns are dedicated to praying and propagating the Perpetual Rosary. Their guiding light in this is St Louis Marie de Montfort. A first principle for them in their work of prayer is taken from Montfort's '*True Devotion*' (No.50), "whosoever will find Mary will find Life, that is Jesus Christ Who is the Way, the Truth and the Life." The method of praying the Rosary by the nuns follows the model of Montfort: to pray for the fruit of each Rosary Mystery. And if one prays the Rosary in the chapel of the nuns at St Pius XII Monastery, Fatima, proclaimed on the sanctuary arch will be seen Montfort's instructive dictum: *Ad Jesum per Mariam*.

### Modern Parochial Influence

The influence of St Louis Marie de Montfort can be found in seemingly unlikely places, including parishes in the UK. In Blackburn at St Peter's Church, for example, a small shrine was set up to the Saint as it was connected with the family of Sr Gerard of the 'canonisation miracle' at the La Sagesse Convent in Romsey, and Sr Gerard herself kept a lifelong interest in the church. But somewhat older than this is the devotion to Our Lady of Light at the Church of that name in Clacton-on-Sea. Devotion to Our Lady of Light can be traced back to Montfort in Brittany in the early 18th Century. The devotion was brought to a small chapel in Cornwall in 1834 by a family that had lived in Brittany, and in turn this little shrine was transferred to Clacton with the permission of Cardinal Vaughan in 1895. This same Cardinal, we saw above, when Bishop of Salford, sent

Montfort's *True Devotion To Mary* to every priest in his diocese. A house was bought near the church and renamed 'Montfort'. For a hundred years, the Montfort-inspired Feast of Our Lady of Light has been celebrated around this seaside church on the first Sunday after the Ascension.

## Pope John Paul II at the Tomb of St Louis Marie de Montfort

The Holy Father visited the tombs of St Louis Marie de Montfort and Blessed Marie Louise Trichet at Saint-Laurent-sur-Sevre on 19 September 1996. He had revealed previously how important the '*True Devotion*' was in his life. " The reading of of this book was a decisive turning-point in my life. I say 'turning-point', but in fact it was a long inner journey......This 'perfect devotion' is indispensable to anyone who means to give himself without reserve to Christ and to the work of redemption." Addressing members of the Orders linked to St Louis Marie his message was: " it is from Montfort that I have taken my motto '*totus tuus*'. Someday I'll have to tell you Montfortians how I discovered de Montfort's *Treatise on True Devotion* and how often I had to re-read it to understand it."

He knelt at the tombs on his visit and then said to the people in the church: "you know that I am very indebted to this Saint and to his *Treatise on True Devotion to the*

**Pope John Paul II visits the tomb of St Louis Marie de Montfort**

*Blessed Virgin.* Today because my pastoral visit has for the most part as its theme the sacrament of baptism, I would like to highlight the fact that, in the mind of St Louis, the whole spiritual life flows directly from the sacrament of holy baptism, as is shown by an important passage in the Act of Consecration to Jesus by the hands of Mary, written in his own precise wording."[5]

## Other Popes on the Work of St Louis Marie de Montfort

Pope Pius IX stated that Montfort's devotion to Mary was the best and most acceptable form of devotion to Our Lady. Pope Leo XIII, who beatified Montfort in 1888, granted a plenary indulgence to those who make his Act of Consecration to Jesus through Mary. On his deathbed he renewed the Act himself and invoked the heavenly aid of Bl. Louis Marie de Montfort. Pope St Pius X declared " I heartily recommend *True Devotion to the Blessed Virgin*, so admirably written by Blessed de Montfort, and to all who read it grant the Apostolic Benediction." Pope Pius XI said "I have practised this devotion ever since my youth." Pope Paul VI declared "we are convinced without any doubt that devotion to Our Lady is essentially

[5] The Act of Consecration: Consecration to Jesus Christ, the Incarnate Wisdom through the Blessed Virgin Mary follows the final point, No.273, in Montfort's Treatise, in a Supplement recommending a substantial Preparation for Consecration.

joined with devotion to Christ, that it assures a firmness of conviction to faith in Him and in His Church, a vital adherence to Him and to His Church which, without devotion to Mary, would be impoverished and compromised."

**ACKNOWLEDGEMENTS**

My grateful thanks to Sr Mildred of the Daughters of Wisdom for her ready kindness in providing information on the work of the Sisters of La Sagesse, and the Order's contribution to the canonisation of St Louis Marie de Montfort.

To Fr Paul Allerton SMM, of the Company of Mary, for his patience, advice and clarification over numerous details of the life of Montfort, and enlightenment as to further references for study.

To Br Daniel Faivre of the Brothers of St Gabriel for his generous help in giving a picture of a hundred years of service of the work of the S.G.s in England, and of the continuing work of the Brothers worldwide.

# BIBLIOGRAPHY


## By St Louis Marie de Montfort

The Love of Eternal Wisdom

True Devotion to Mary
(Treatise on the True Devotion to the Blessed Virgin)

The Secret of Mary

The Secret of the Rosary
(The Admirable Secret of the Rosary)

The Letter to the Friends of the Cross

Prayer for Missionaries

## Of St Louis Marie de Montfort

Montfort Press, Liverpool, *God Alone, The Collected Writing of St Louis Marie de Montfort*

Bolger E.C. SMM, *The Man Called Montfort*

Doherty, Eddie, *Wisdom's Fool*

Papasogli, Benedetta, *Montfort. A Prophet for our Times*

Sr St Mildred of Lourdes, FDLS, *Ticket To Heaven*